I0530001

Transforming
Team Relationships
From the Inside Out

The SWEET Healing Circle for Agencies: Redefining
Accountability, Collaboration, and Culture

Mardoche Sidor, MD | Alison Dockery, PhD

Karen Dubin, PhD, LCSW | SWEET Institute

SWEET Institute Publishing
Transformational Books for a Transformational World

Published by:

SWEET Institute Publishing
New York, NY
WWW.SWEETInstitutePublishing.com

First Edition
Printed in the United States of America

ISBN (Paperback): [978-1-968105-02-0]

Cover Design: [SWEET Institute Publishing]
Interior Design and Layout: [SWEET Institute Publishing]

For bulk orders, permissions, or media inquiries, please contact:
info@sweetinstitutepublishing.com

SWEET Institute Publishing
Transformational Books for a Transformational World

Dedication

To every staff member who has stayed late, showed up tired, given your all, and still wondered if it was enough—This book is for you.

To the supervisors who carry invisible burdens and still lead with compassion—This book is for you.

To the directors and executives who know that culture is more than policy, and who dare to model reflection, humility, and hope—This book is for you.

To the courageous souls who have sat in Circle, told the truth, taken a breath, and chosen to heal—You are the reason we keep going.

And to the next generation of agencies, may you be places of justice, dignity, courage, and care—From the inside out.

With deepest respect,

Mardoche Sidor, MD
Alison Dockery, PhD
Karen Dubin, PhD, LCSW
SWEET Institute

Other Books by Mardoche Sidor, M.D; Karen Dubin, PhD, LCSW; with the SWEET Institute

- Journey to Empowerment
- Discovering Your Worth: Everything You Need to Feel Fulfilled
- The Power of Faith: A Harvard-Trained Psychiatrist Speaking on Faith
- The Psychotherapy Certificate Course: The Clinician and Coach Manual (Books 1–3)
- The Anxiety Course: The Workbook
- What's Missing
- NLP for Clinicians
- 50 SWEET Poems: Reflections on life, love and self
- The Power of Belief: How Ideas Shape Leaders, Nations and the Future
- The Courage to Care: Stories of Healing, Hope, and the Power of Social Work: Told by Over 50 SWEET Institute Social Workers

Table of Contents

Foreword
By Iverson Bell Jr., MD, DLFAPA

Associate Professor of Psychiatry
Former Residency Training Director, UT Health Science Center

In over four decades of psychiatric education and leadership, I have witnessed countless approaches to improve workplace culture, clinician resilience, and team effectiveness. Most begin with good intentions. Many are well-designed. A few create meaningful shifts.

But rare is the model that combines depth psychology, systems thinking, and practical transformation in a scientifically grounded and profoundly human way.

The SWEET Healing Circle is one of those rare models.

I have long believed that the relational environment within our institutions is just as important as the clinical interventions we provide. How we treat one another behind closed doors ultimately affects how we treat the individuals we serve. Burnout, staff turnover, and team conflict are not signs of weakness but signs of systems that have not yet learned how to heal themselves.

This book arrives at a time when healing is no longer optional.

With clarity, humility, and conviction, the authors walk us through the why, the how, and the what-next of healing institutional relationships from the inside out. They challenge us to move beyond the surface of professionalism and into the heart of self-awareness, responsibility, and reflection. They offer not just theory but structure — a rhythm of breath, pause, dialogue, and recommitment that has already been able to shift teams across agencies, across disciplines, and across the country.

This is not a book about making staff feel better. It's about making systems work better by starting where all healing begins: with ourselves.

As a medical educator and leader, I see in this work an invitation to every administrator, supervisor, and clinician to pause — to ask not just "What are we doing wrong?" but "What is ready to change in me, in us, in our way of being together?"

If you are open to that question, this book will not disappoint. It may even transform you.

Iverson Bell Jr., MD, DLFAPA

Associate Professor of Psychiatry
Former Residency Training Director

Preface

By Mardoche Sidor, MD

Assistant Clinical Professor of Psychiatry (Former), Columbia University
Columbia University Center for Psychoanalytic Study and Research (Current)

I didn't set out to create a healing circle. I set out to respond to pain — the kind that didn't show up in symptom checklists or outcome dashboards. The kind that sat silently in the staff lounge. That lingered after meetings. That was carried, quietly and heavily, by the very people we count on to help others heal.

For years, I watched good clinicians leave agencies not because they lacked skill or dedication, but because the environment became too toxic to breathe in. I watched leaders lead from exhaustion instead of vision. I listened to teams who loved their mission but had lost trust in each other. And I kept asking myself: What's missing?

We train for clinical skills, but not for relational repair. We train for documentation, but not for dialogue. We train for outcomes, but rarely for ownership. We teach self-care — but not system care.

That's where the idea for the SWEET Healing Circle was born. Not from a manual. Not from theory. But from a lived recognition that we needed a new way to be together. A way to reflect without judgment. To speak honestly. To witness one another. To reconnect with the meaning behind the mission.

The Healing Circle is not a group therapy session. It's not a training. It's not a feel-good intervention. It is a structured, layered, and psychologically-informed process that helps individuals, teams, and entire agencies begin to see clearly — and choose consciously — how they want to relate, lead, and serve.

It is built on science, story, and a deep respect for the complexity of human systems.

This book is an offering of that process. It contains what we've learned from years of running Circles across agencies — from hospital systems to community health to executive leadership. It brings together the four layers that shape all sustainable change: the conscious, the pre-conscious, the unconscious, and the existential. And it reminds us that what happens between us at work is never just about the work.

You don't need to finish this book in one sitting. But I encourage you to sit with it. Pause after each chapter. Reflect. Share it with your team. Try the tools. More than anything, let this book be a mirror — and a map. Because I've come to believe that the most important systems we can ever transform are the ones we are a part of.

If you're reading this, it means you care. You care enough to look inward. You care enough to stay curious. You care enough to begin. Let this book be your companion as you do just that.

With deep respect,

Mardoche Sidor, MD
Assistant Clinical Professor of Psychiatry (Former), Columbia University
Columbia University Center for Psychoanalytic Study and Research (Current)
Founder, SWEET Institute
Medical Director, Urban Pathways

Introduction

From the Authors

From Mardoche Sidor, MD

We live in a time when burnout has become normalized, when disconnection is mistaken for professionalism, and when the people responsible for healing others often have the least space to heal themselves.

I've worked across systems long enough to know this isn't a personal failure — it's a structural one. But I've also come to understand something deeper: the structure doesn't shift until the people within it begin to.

That's what the SWEET Healing Circle is all about. It's not a training. It's not a morale booster. It's not a one-time retreat. It's a repeatable, relationship-based, psychologically-informed process that helps individuals and systems move from reactivity to responsibility, from pattern to presence, from surface-level compliance to meaningful change.

This book offers that process to you — wherever you are in your agency or your leadership. We built it from years of practice, reflection, and dialogue. It brings together science, lived experience, group process, and real transformation across the four layers of healing: the conscious, pre-conscious, unconscious, and existential.

You don't have to be a clinician to use this book. You just have to care. About people. About culture. About doing work that honors your purpose — and the people around you.

Start with one chapter. Try one tool. Have one conversation. Then watch what shifts — inside you, and around you.

Welcome to the Circle.

— Mardoche Sidor, MD

From Karen Dubin, PhD, LCSW

As a social worker, educator, supervisor, and leader, I've long believed that healing is relational. That what we avoid in others is often what we haven't yet faced in ourselves. And that systems reflect the inner worlds of the people inside them.

What I've seen in the Healing Circles — what I've witnessed again and again — is the moment when someone realizes that the person triggering them is actually showing them something about themselves. It's raw. It's humbling. But it's the beginning of change.

This book is filled with those moments. And it doesn't stop at awareness — it moves toward accountability, choice, and growth. Each chapter is layered, with story, science, and tools. You'll find reflection questions, real scripts, and pathways for integration.

Use it in supervision. Bring it to your team. Bring it to yourself.

This is how systems heal — one reflection at a time.

— Karen Dubin, PhD, LCSW

From Alison Dockery, PhD

I've worked with leaders across sectors who want the same thing: less conflict, more collaboration, and a culture that actually supports the people who do the work. But most of those leaders are stuck — not because they don't care, but because they don't know where to begin.

This book offers a beginning. It shows how to shift culture through structure. How to make reflection a habit. How to create spaces where people feel safe enough to show up with honesty, humility, and hope.

The SWEET Healing Circle is powerful because it's repeatable. It's layered, grounded, and practical. And it's designed to be with teams where they are — whether they're in crisis or on the cusp of something new.

This is a book about systems, yes — but more than that, it's about people. It's about how we relate, and how we repair.

Read it with your team. Reflect with it in leadership meetings. Let it be a tool for growth — not just for your agency, but for you.

— Alison Dockery, PhD

Why This Book

Because staff are exhausted — not just by the work, but by how we work together. Because agencies are struggling with turnover, burnout, and team conflict, and the solutions offered have not touched the root. Because we've been trained to perform, produce, and protect ourselves — but rarely to pause, reflect, relate, and repair. Because culture doesn't shift through compliance. It shifts through consciousness.

Because leadership is not just about strategy. It's about presence. Because even the best policies fail when people don't feel safe. Because what happens between us — in supervision, in meetings, in conflict — is where transformation begins. Because we need more than information. We need integration.

Because healing is not just for our clients. It's for us too. Because the Circle is not a concept — it is a practice, a mirror, a movement.

This book was written to offer what so many systems are missing:

- A structure for reflection
- A method for healing
- A culture of accountability
- And a way forward, from the inside out.

We wrote this book because you — your teams, your leaders, your mission — deserve more than survival. You deserve to heal, grow, and lead in a system that supports transformation, not burnout. That system begins here. With you.

This book is your invitation.

What This Book Is About

This book is about healing systems — by transforming relationships. It introduces the SWEET Healing Circle for Agencies, a science-based, relationship-centered, trauma-informed model that helps teams shift from disconnection, conflict, and burnout to collaboration, accountability, and meaning.

This is not just a guide for how to improve staff morale or reduce turnover — though it will help do both. It is a step-by-step framework for how to create a culture where people feel seen, supported, and responsible for how they show up with one another.

Rooted in SWEET's Four-Layer Model of Transformation — Conscious, Pre-Conscious, Unconscious, and Existential — this book:

- Offers a full blueprint for running effective Healing Circles
- Provides real stories, scientific insights, tools, and reflection practices
- Bridges the gap between intellectual learning and lasting behavior change
- Helps leaders and teams embody healing, not just talk about it
- Centers the belief that systems don't change until people within them do

Whether you're a supervisor, clinician, team member, executive, or organizational leader, this book is designed to support you in:

- Understanding your own patterns
- Supporting others with clarity and care
- Building trust within teams
- Repairing what has been fractured
- And reconnecting your work with your deeper "why"

This book is about reclaiming the soul of our workplaces — one Circle at a time.

How This Book Came About

This book didn't begin with a theory. It began with tension; with repeated moments of frustration across teams; with brilliant staff leaving organizations because of conflict they couldn't name, let alone resolve; with leaders trying every possible training — and still wondering why nothing was sticking.

It came from my own experience as a psychiatrist, educator, and Medical Director — sitting in meetings where people were expected to be "professional," but couldn't be human.

From watching supervisors struggle to lead while carrying invisible wounds. From listening to staff who knew what needed to change — but didn't feel safe enough to say it. It came from years of trying to teach accountability without shame, reflection without fear, and collaboration without burnout. And it originates from a truth that all three of us hold dear: The system can't heal if the people inside it are suffering.

At SWEET, we began to ask better questions. What if we created a structured space — not for performance, but for presence? What if staff had time to reflect on their patterns, not just their productivity? What if healing was possible — even inside a system that often feels like it's moving too fast to care?

That's when the Healing Circle was born. It started quietly — with one team, one room, one breath. Then it spread — to peer specialists, clinicians, nurses, directors, administrators. It reached the staff that most systems overlook — and the leaders who had run out of tools. It didn't take long to realize: this wasn't just helpful. It was necessary.

We wrote this book because so many teams were asking: What can we do for our agency? What can we do ourselves? How can we build a culture around this?

This book is your guide, your companion, and your map. It's rooted in science, but it's also rooted in people, in real conversations, real tension, real healing. It came from the field. And it was written for you.

How to Use This Book

This book is not meant to be read once and shelved. It's meant to be used, revisited, practiced, and shared. You don't have to read it cover to cover before applying what's inside. In fact, the sooner you begin using the tools and prompts, the more transformational this book becomes.

Here's how to get the most out of it:

1. Read with a highlighter — and a mirror.

This book is filled with prompts, patterns, and reflections. Highlight what resonates. Pause often. Let the book reveal not just new ideas, but parts of yourself.

2. Reflect individually, then bring it to your team.

The Healing Circle begins within — but its power multiplies in relationship. Use this book for personal insight and as a tool for team conversations, supervision, or leadership retreats.

3. Use the Reader Integration Toolkit.

In the Appendix, you'll find a set of structured tools, exercises, and planning guides to help you move from insight to action. Use them weekly. Share them. Adapt them to your setting.

4. Start a Circle. Or deepen the one you're in.

Whether you're an agency leader, supervisor, or team member, you can begin. Start with the Circle structure in Chapter 3. Invite others in. You don't need to be perfect. You just need to be willing.

5. Reread as you grow.

Each time you come back to this book, you'll see something new. Because you'll be new. Each layer — conscious, pre-conscious, unconscious, and existential — opens more fully as your awareness expands.

6. Let this book live in conversation.

Bring it to supervision. Quote it in staff meetings. Share a chapter at a team lunch. Healing doesn't happen in isolation — it happens in relationship. You don't need to "finish" the book to begin. You only need to take the next step. One breath. One practice. One conversation at a time.

How This Book Works

This book was designed not just to inform you, but to transform the way you relate, lead, and collaborate — from the inside out.

Each chapter follows a structure based on the SWEET Healing Circle methodology, built on the Four Layers of Transformation: Conscious, Pre-Conscious, Unconscious, and Existential.

You'll find a consistent rhythm:

1. Story and Scene
Every chapter begins with a real-life moment: a staff conversation, a leadership turning point, or a Circle insight. These vignettes ground the work in lived experience.

2. Core Concepts and Science
Next, you'll explore the psychological, organizational, and behavioral principles that underlie the issue at hand — backed by research, theory, and practice.

3. The Four Layers in Action
You'll be guided through the issue using SWEET's Four-Layer Model:

- Conscious Layer – Observable behaviors and habits
- Pre-Conscious Layer – Unseen patterns and beliefs
- Unconscious Layer – Repressed dynamics and emotional histories
- Existential Layer – Meaning, purpose, and choice

This framework helps you see the full picture — not just what's happening, but why.

4. Tools, Reflections, and Practices
Each chapter includes:

- Reflection prompts to personalize the insights
- Exercises and worksheets for integration
- Commitment practices to apply the learning right away
- Infographics or tables for visual clarity and accessibility

5. Scientific References
At the end of each chapter, you'll find real scientific citations to support further learning and credibility — bridging clinical depth with practical application.

This book is modular — each chapter can stand alone or be used in sequence. You can read it cover to cover, or start with the chapter most relevant to your current challenge.

Whether you're using it as a guide for personal growth, team transformation, or agency-wide implementation, this book was built to meet you where you are — and help you lead from there.

Front Acknowledgments

We offer our deepest thanks to the clinicians and staff, who have participated in the SWEET Healing Circle and other SWEET offerings. Your courage to reflect, your willingness to grow, and your commitment to healing, not only in others, but in yourselves, are the foundation of this book.

To the agencies and leaders who opened their doors and their hearts to this work: thank you for believing in transformation.

To our SWEET community — members, facilitators, mentors, pioneers, and vision-bearers — your light has shaped every word on these pages.

May this book honor your work and reflect your wisdom.

— **Karen Dubin, PhD, LCSW**
— **Mardoche Sidor, MD**
— **Alison Dockery, PhD**
— **SWEET Institute**

Part I

The Case for Change

Chapter 1 — The Staff Are Not Okay

Why burnout, conflict, and disconnection are symptoms of a deeper system problem

"We don't rise to the level of our mission. We fall to the level of our relationships." — SWEET Institute

Scene: Tuesday Morning, 9:04 a.m.

Carla, a program director, stood outside her office gripping a mug she hadn't sipped. She'd already rewritten an email three times to her supervisor. Her body was there. Her mind was exhausted. Her heart? Disconnected.

Inside the conference room, Mike, a senior case manager, sat slumped over the monthly incident report. Another psychiatric decompensation. Another staff conflict. Another coworker quitting.

"Again?" he thought. "How is this still happening?"

Moments later, Carla walked in.

Carla: "Mike, we need to talk about Friday."

Mike: (tight voice) "About Jason?"

Carla: "Yes. But also, about how the team responded. There was no coordination."

Mike: "I was dealing with a screaming client and two new hires panicking. What did you want me to do?"

Carla: "I'm not blaming you—"

Mike: "You never are. But somehow, it's always on me."

A long silence.

The Unspoken Reality

These aren't isolated incidents. They are symptoms of a deeper, systemic wound that no compliance training, no new EHR system, no pizza party will fix.

The truth? The staff are not okay. They're tired, triggered, quietly checked out. And they don't always know why.

What we're witnessing across agencies is a slow erosion of morale, unity, and meaning. Not because people are lazy. But because the relational foundation is broken.

When the relationships falter, the mission shakes.

The Science of Burnout, Turnover, and Disconnection

According to the World Health Organization (WHO), burnout is a syndrome resulting from chronic workplace stress that has not been successfully managed. Its hallmarks: exhaustion, cynicism, and reduced professional efficacy.

In human services, burnout rates can exceed 60%, especially when emotional labor is high and recognition is low (Maslach et al., 2001; APA, 2022).

But beneath the statistics lies something more subtle: relationship fatigue — the weariness that comes not from the work itself, but from how people treat one another while doing it.

Reflection Prompt

Where is the pain showing up in your team?

In silence? In passive-aggression? In constant crisis? In gossip? In exits?

When staff are not okay, it doesn't always look like absenteeism. Sometimes it looks like compliance without engagement. Sometimes it looks like people protecting themselves from one another.

The 4 Layers of Why It Hurts

To transform, we are to understand why it hurts — and at what level.

1. Conscious Layer

- Staff are sleep-deprived, malnourished, overstimulated.
- They skip lunch, spend the majority of their time in nonessential tasks, and collapse at home.
- They've lost rituals of recovery. They need new structure, boundaries, and self-care habits.

2. Pre-Conscious Layer

- Hidden beliefs drive staff behavior:
    - "If I speak up, I'll be punished."
    - "I have to do everything myself."
    - "Supervisors only care when there's a problem."
- These beliefs come from prior systems, personal history, family roles — and now play out at work.

3. Unconscious Layer

- Past traumas get reactivated by workplace dynamics:
    - Authority figures = threat
    - Conflict = abandonment
    - Criticism = humiliation
- Without awareness, these echoes shape every interaction.
- Teams repeat roles unconsciously: the fixer, the avoider, the scapegoat.

4. Existential Layer

- Beneath it all, staff wonder: Why am I even here?
  - They've lost meaning.
  - They forgot their "why."
  - Or no one ever asked them.
- Without reconnection to purpose, work becomes mechanical — or unbearable.

The Invitation

We begin here because healing doesn't start with a strategy. It starts with a reckoning.

The staff are not okay. But they can be. Not by being told what to do. But by being invited into a new experience of each other — and of themselves.

That's what the SWEET Healing Circle for Relationships does. It brings the team together. Not to perform. But to see. Not to vent. But to understand. Not to blame. But to begin again — with honesty, clarity, and hope.

SIGNS OF SURFACE FUNCTIONING VS. HEALING CULTURE

SURFACE FUNCTIONING	HEALING CULTURE
• Staff comply, but don't care	• Staff engage and take ownership
• Conflict is avoided	• Conflict is explored and healed
• "Us vs. Them" thinking	• Shared mission across levels
• High Turnover	• High Belonging
• Stress is normalized	• Recovery is modeled and honored.

Tool: The Relationship Pulse Check

Use this tool to check where your team is:

- Rate your team (1–10):

RELATIONAL PULSE CHECK

Description	Rating (1-10)
Trust Among Co-Workers	
Psychological Safety	
Clarity of Communication	
Ability to Repair After Conflict	
Shared Ownership of Outcomes	

- Reflect: Which area needs healing first?

Commitment Practice

This week, choose one person on your team who you tend to judge or avoid.

Pause. Reflect. Ask yourself:

- What if their behavior is a mirror for something unresolved in me?
- What happens if I stop reacting and start getting curious?

Then: practice one small act of engagement — a check-in, a "thank you," or a moment of listening without fixing.

That's how healing begins.

Scientific References

- Maslach, C., Jackson, S. E., & Leiter, M. P. (2001). Job burnout. Annual Review of Psychology, 52(1), 397–422.
- American Psychological Association (2022). Workforce wellbeing survey.
- Edmondson, A. (1999). Psychological safety and learning behavior in work teams. Administrative Science Quarterly, 44(2), 350–383.
- Jung, C. G. (1959). The Archetypes and the Collective Unconscious. Princeton University Press.
- Van der Kolk, B. (2014). The Body Keeps the Score. Viking.

Chapter 2 — Conflict Is Not the Problem

How the stories we carry shape the relationships we build — and break

"It's not what happened. It's what it touched inside of me." — SWEET Institute

Scene: Wednesday Afternoon, 3:17 p.m.

Tasha, a clinician, slammed the file drawer shut. Her knuckles were white. Across the room, Rafi, a care coordinator, scrolled silently on his phone.

Tasha: "You still haven't logged that progress note, and it's affecting my discharge summary."

Rafi: (without looking up) "You could've just reminded me nicely."

Tasha: "Excuse me?"

Rafi: "The way you speak to people — no wonder there's always drama with you."

Tasha: "Oh, so now I'm the drama?"

Rafi: "If the shoe fits…"

Silence. Again.

Two coworkers. Two histories. A spark turned to fire.

Not because of the content — but because of the unseen context.

The Myth of Conflict

In many agencies, the moment conflict arises, the impulse is to shut it down. Redirect. Escalate. Mediate. Reassign. But here's the truth: Conflict is not the problem. Unprocessed emotion is. Unexamined projection is. Unconscious pattern repetition is.

The real damage isn't caused by disagreement. It's caused by reactivity without awareness — the automatic reenactment of old wounds dressed in workplace clothes.

The Neuroscience of Reactivity

When triggered, the brain activates the amygdala — our fight-flight-freeze response. In that moment, we're not reasoning. We're protecting. Studies show that even minor workplace slights can provoke threat responses similar to physical danger (Lieberman et al., 2007).

Why? Because rejection and exclusion trigger the same brain regions as pain. This is why conflict escalates fast — not because of the present, but because of the past it reactivates.

The Psychology of Projection

Carl Jung famously wrote: "Everything that irritates us about others can lead us to an understanding of ourselves." This is projection — when we unconsciously disown parts of ourselves and see them exaggerated in others.

- Tasha's tone touched Rafi's wound of disrespect.
- Rafi's dismissal touched Tasha's wound of being unseen.
- Neither saw the other. Both saw themselves reflected back — and flinched.
- Conflict, in this light, becomes a mirror — not a battlefield.

Reflection Prompt

- Who triggers you at work?
- What about them irritates you the most?

- When else in your life have you felt this way?
- What part of yourself might you be seeing in them?

When we become curious, conflict becomes growth.

The Four Layers Applied to Conflict

1. Conscious Layer

- Observable behavior: eye rolls, sarcasm, avoidance, emails with edge
- Tools needed: communication skills, de-escalation techniques, body awareness
- Healing Circle practice: breath check, labeling emotion before speaking

2. Pre-Conscious Layer

- Core beliefs: "I'm not safe," "People don't respect me," "I always have to defend myself"
- Triggered scripts from past experiences
- Healing Circle practice: identifying repeated conflict themes

3. Unconscious Layer

- Repressed hurts: old humiliation, abandonment, injustice
- Transference dynamics: authority figures, sibling rivalry, parental echoes
- Healing Circle practice: free association, dream reflection, symbolic inquiry

4. Existential Layer

- Questions of meaning: "Why am I here?" "Who do I choose to be?"
- Choosing accountability, presence, and purpose over reaction
- Healing Circle practice: aligning responses with mission, values, and vision

Dialogue Revisited (With Awareness)

What if Tasha and Rafi had gone through a Healing Circle?

Tasha: "I noticed I felt really activated just now. I want to pause before I react."

Rafi: "Same. I think I took your tone personally, but I know that's mine to work on."

Tasha: "Let's reset. I want us to be a team — not enemies."

Rafi: "Me too."

CONFLICT AS A MIRROR, NOT A THREAT

Trigger	Possible Projection	Underlying Wound
"They don't listen"	I don't feel heard	Childhood dismissal
"They're always judging"	I'm judging myself	Shame, perfectionism
They're incompetent	I fear being exposed as unworthy	Imposter syndrome
"They're lazy"	I push myself too hard	Over-responsibility, burnout

Tool: The Conflict Inquiry Template

Next time you're triggered, pause and ask:

1. What exactly did I feel?
2. What was I thinking?
3. Where else in my life have I felt this way?
4. What belief might this be activating?
5. What do I want to choose now?

This tool shifts the focus from blaming others to understanding ourselves.

Commitment Practice

This week, choose one moment of conflict — past or present.

Journal using the Conflict Inquiry Template.

Then practice one non-reactive response in your next challenging interaction.

Maybe it's silence. Maybe it's curiosity. Maybe it's a pause.

That pause may save a relationship.

That pause may begin healing.

Scientific References

- Lieberman, M. D., & Eisenberger, N. I. (2007). The neural bases of social pain: evidence for shared representations with physical pain. Nature Reviews Neuroscience, 8(3), 203–212.
- Jung, C. G. (1959). The Archetypes and the Collective Unconscious. Princeton University Press.
- Yalom, I. D. (1995). The Theory and Practice of Group Psychotherapy. Basic Books.
- Siegel, D. J. (2007). The Mindful Brain. Norton & Company.
- Gross, J. J. (2014). Emotion regulation: Conceptual foundations. Handbook of Emotion Regulation (2nd ed.).

Chapter 3 — The SWEET Healing Circle Model

What it is, how it works, and why it's transforming the way teams relate

"Culture doesn't change when people are told what to do. It changes when people experience a new way of being together." — SWEET Institute

Scene: Friday Morning, 9:51 a.m.

Malika, a senior director, sat at the back of the conference room, arms crossed.

To her left was Jacob, a housing coordinator known for being skeptical of anything "touchy-feely."

To her right, Camille, a peer specialist, tapped her pen nervously.

Twelve team members were in the room. Two had already asked, "What exactly is this?"

The SWEET Healing Circle was about to begin.

No one quite knew what to expect.

Facilitator (Karen): "We're not here to be told what to do. We're here to see what's getting in the way — together."

Jacob: "So, this isn't a training?"

Karen: "No. This is an experience."

There was a long silence. Then the circle began.

What Is the SWEET Healing Circle?

The SWEET Healing Circle for Relationships is a structured, science-informed, emotionally safe space where agency staff experience:

1. Insight into their own relational patterns
2. Connection with one another beyond roles and labels
3. Choice — to shift from blame to ownership, from reaction to responsibility

It's based on decades of research in:

- Group process (Yalom, 1995)
- Interpersonal neurobiology (Siegel, 2007)
- Adult learning (Kolb, 1984)
- Organizational behavior (Schein, 2010)
- Psychodynamic theory and schema models

The Circle isn't just educational — it's transformational.

Structure of the Circle

Total Time: 5 Hours

Number of Participants: 10–20 staff

Facilitators: 1–2 SWEET-trained professionals

CIRCLE AGENDA

Time	Section
10:00-10:30am	Welcome + Grounding + Agreements
10:30-11:30am	Part I: Discovering Patterns in Our Work Relationships
11:30-12:10pm	Part II: How Our Patterns Are Hindering Collaboration
12:10-12:30pm	Break
12:30-1:30pm	Part III: The Missing Link – Why Things Haven't Changed
1:30-2:30pm	Part IV: A New Way of Relating to Ourselves and One Another
2:30-3:00pm	Debrief + One Commitment

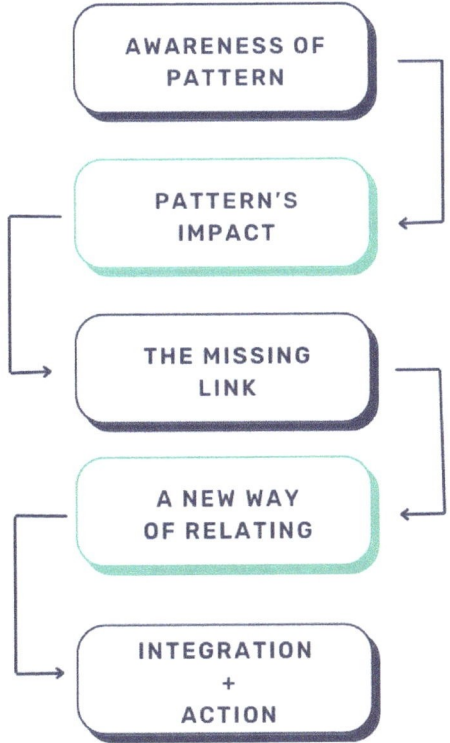

Each layer builds on the one before — slowly shifting perception, ownership, and behavior.

Science Behind the Model

1. Experiential Learning

(Kolb, 1984)

People change when they experience insight — not when they're told.

2. Neuroplasticity

(Doidge, 2007)

When staff reflect on a pattern, pause before reacting, and reframe it — they literally rewire neural pathways.

3. Polyvagal Theory

(Porges, 2011)

The Circle fosters co-regulation: when people feel seen and heard in safe, non-judgmental environments, their nervous systems settle — allowing reflection and choice.

4. Group Process & Universality

(Yalom, 1995)

When staff realize they're not alone in their struggle — healing begins.

What the Circle Is Not

- Not therapy
- Not a performance review
- Not a venting session
- Not a policy change meeting

It's a transformational space grounded in evidence, held with dignity, and designed for agency growth.

Reflection Prompt

What would it take for your staff to feel safe enough to be real with one another?

What might your agency gain if your people trusted each other more deeply?

FROM TRAINING TO TRANSFORMATION

Traditional Training	SWEET Healing Circle
Information download	Experiential insight
One-way communication	Dialogue + Inquiry
Skill-based only	Identity-based + relational
No accountability	Peer-supported commitment
Cognitive only	Cognitive + emotional + behavioral

What Staff Experience

- Relief — "I'm not the only one."
- Insight — "I've been reacting based on something I wasn't even aware of."
- Reconnection — "I remembered why I came into this field."
- Responsibility — "I'm choosing to show up differently."
- Hope — "We can do this — together."

Tool: The Circle Commitment Card

At the end of the Circle, each staff member commits to:

1. One new pattern they will stop engaging in
2. One way they will practice accountability
3. One relationship they will invest in repairing
4. One belief they are ready to release
5. One reminder of why they do this work

They can keep the card, carry it, post it, or share it with a colleague.

Commitment Practice

If you're a leader, take a moment to ask yourself:

- What pattern do I model that may be contributing to reactivity or disconnection on my team?
- What would it mean for me to enter a Circle as a participant, not a position?

Leadership begins with self-reflection.

Scientific References

- Kolb, D. A. (1984). Experiential learning: Experience as the source of learning and development.
- Doidge, N. (2007). The Brain That Changes Itself. Penguin.
- Porges, S. W. (2011). The Polyvagal Theory. Norton.
- Yalom, I. D. (1995). The Theory and Practice of Group Psychotherapy. Basic Books.
- Siegel, D. J. (2007). The Mindful Brain. Norton & Company.
- Schein, E. H. (2010). Organizational Culture and Leadership. Jossey-Bass.

Part II

The Framework for Transformation

Chapter 4 — The Four Layers of Transformation

Conscious. Pre-conscious. Unconscious. Existential. The complete map for personal and systemic change

"Lasting change only happens when we descend through the mind and rise through the soul." — SWEET Institute

Scene: End of the Circle — 2:48 p.m.

Camille, the peer specialist who'd been quiet all day, finally spoke.

Camille: "At first, I didn't think this was for me. But now I see… I've been trying to change things at the surface. And the truth is, it's not just the job that's exhausting me. It's me. My patterns. My stories. My wounds." "I just… I want to live differently. And I didn't know that was even an option until now."

Silence.

Then tears.

Then something rare: integration.

The Problem With Surface Change

Most staff are given surface solutions to deep-rooted problems:

- Time management for unspoken overwhelm
- Communication training for emotional reactivity
- Wellness webinars for identity-level burnout

But true transformation is not a single-layered event.

It's a multi-layered journey — through the mind, into the body, and down to the soul.

44

At SWEET, we call this the Topographical Model of Transformation.

THE FOUR LAYERS: AN OVERVIEW

Layer	Focus	Primary Mode	Healing Approaches
Conscious	Behavior, habits, structure	Willpower, discipline	Routines, schedules, breathwork, lifestyle changes, coaching, CBT
Pre-Conscious	Patterns, schemas, attachments	Awareness + reflection	Schema Therapy, ACT, Gestalt, mindfulness, inner child work
Unconscious	Repressed experiences, defenses	Free association, Symbols	Dream work, psychodynamic work, interpretation, trauma resolution
Existential	Meaning, purpose, freedom, choice	Integration + vision	Existential therapy, values work, responsibility, spiritual reflection, golden rule

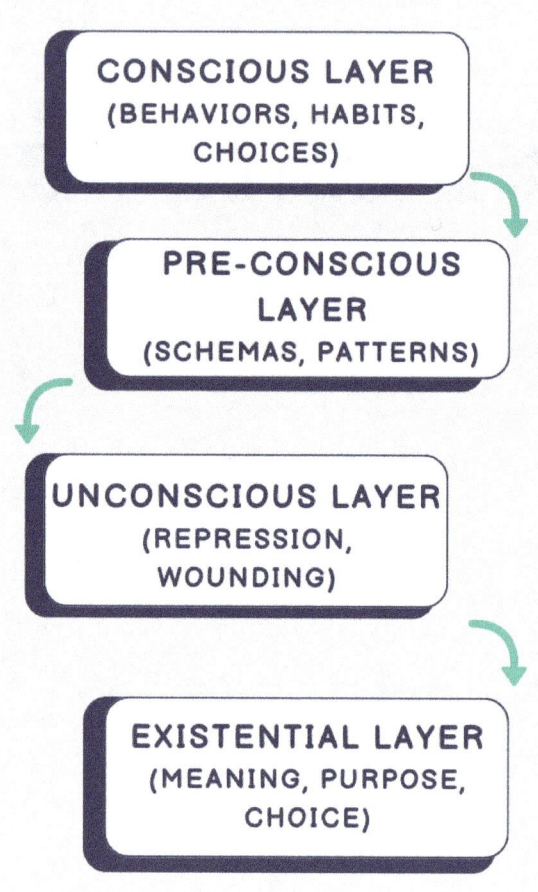

Layer 1: Conscious — The Realm of Action

This is where most trainings stop — and where all change begins.

Staff are supported to:

- Adjust schedules and habits
- Improve sleep and nutrition
- Learn breathwork and regulation tools
- Set new goals and build new accountability systems

But without deeper work, change here is fragile. Without healing what drives behavior, motivation fades.

Circle Practice: Mindful breathing, body check-ins, intention setting

Sample Prompt: What habit is no longer serving your highest self?

Layer 2: Pre-Conscious — The Realm of Pattern

Here live the schemas — belief systems that once protected us but now keep us stuck.

- "I'm only valuable when I overwork."
- "If I speak up, I'll be rejected."
- "No one's coming to help me."

These beliefs often go unchallenged. They drive our reactivity, sabotage our growth, and strain relationships.

Circle Practice: Noticing repeated themes in conflict

Sample Prompt: What story are you unconsciously repeating at work?

Healing Modalities Used:

- Schema Therapy
- ACT (Acceptance and Commitment Therapy)
- Mindfulness and Gestalt techniques

Layer 3: Unconscious — The Realm of Repression

Here we find what's buried — traumas, emotions, parts of ourselves we've disowned.

These often show up indirectly:

- Transference onto supervisors
- Sabotage of supportive relationships
- Fear of authority rooted in past betrayal

Healing this layer requires slowness, safety, and symbol — not instruction.

Circle Practice: Symbolic inquiry, dream exploration, noticing emotional charge

Sample Prompt: What's trying to be heard through your resistance?

Healing Modalities Used:

- Psychodynamic exploration
- Free association
- Internal Family Systems
- Dream work

Layer 4: Existential — The Realm of Meaning and Freedom

Here lies the final question:

"Now that I am aware… who do I choose to become?"

This is the layer where healing becomes integration.

Staff reconnect with:

- Their personal "why"
- Their right to choose
- Their power to respond
- Their ability to build meaningful lives through service

Circle Practice: Purpose journaling, value mapping, shared vision building

Sample Prompt: What legacy are you building in the lives of the people you serve — and in your own?

Philosophical Roots:

- Viktor Frankl's Logotherapy
- Existentialism
- The Golden Rule as Ethical Compass

Why the Layers Are to Be Addressed in Sequence

Exploring trauma (unconscious) without building safety and structure (conscious) can be destabilizing.

Making new choices (existential) without understanding patterns (pre-conscious) leads to relapse.

Healing is like descending a staircase — then rising through a new door.

The Descent and Ascent of Change

Descent:

- Conscious (I see my actions)
- Pre-Conscious (I see my patterns)
- Unconscious (I uncover my wounds)

Ascent:

- Existential (I reclaim my power to choose)

Tool: The Four-Layer Self-Assessment Grid

Invite staff to assess themselves at each layer:

THE FOUR LAYER SELF-ASSESSMENT GRID

Layer	How Aware Am I Here?	Scale (1-10)	One Area to Explore
Conscious	E.g., Sleep, Breath		
Pre-Conscious	E.g., Perfectionism		
Unconscious	E.g., Transference		
Existential	E.g., Loss of Purpose		

Use this in supervision, Circle follow-up, or personal journaling.

Commitment Practice

Choose one layer to explore more deeply this week.

- **Conscious**: Commit to one behavior change (e.g., no checking email after 9 p.m.)
- **Pre-conscious**: Journal on a repeating workplace pattern
- **Unconscious**: Record your dreams or track moments of reactivity
- **Existential**: Revisit your personal mission — and write one sentence about why you still choose this work

Scientific References

- Beck, A. T., Freeman, A. (1990). Cognitive Therapy of Personality Disorders. Guilford Press.
- Young, J. E., Klosko, J. S. (2003). Schema Therapy: A Practitioner's Guide. Guilford.
- Freud, S. (1915). The Unconscious. SE, 14: 159–215.
- Frankl, V. E. (1946). Man's Search for Meaning. Beacon Press.
- Yalom, I. D. (1980). Existential Psychotherapy. Basic Books.
- Porges, S. W. (2011). The Polyvagal Theory. Norton.

Chapter 5 — Projection at Work

Why what bothers us most in others is often what's most unhealed in us

"Everything that irritates us about others can lead us to an understanding of ourselves." — Carl Jung

Scene: Post-Circle Debrief, Monday 1:15 p.m.

Tasha, the clinician from Chapter 2, sat across from her supervisor in supervision.

Tasha: "I think I owe Rafi an apology. Not because I was wrong — but because I saw something in him I couldn't face in myself."

Supervisor: "That's powerful. What was it?"

Tasha: "My own avoidance. My own fear of being dismissed. I saw him shut down and it made me furious — because I do the same thing."

She paused. Then added: "The Circle made me realize…we're mirrors. And I've been blaming the reflection."

The Nature of Projection

Projection is an unconscious defense mechanism — a way the mind protects us from discomfort by displacing internal material onto external people.

In the workplace, it looks like this:

- "She's so controlling." (Translation: I fear losing control.)
- "He never listens." (Translation: I feel unheard — often by myself.)
- "They think they're better than everyone." (Translation: I feel inadequate and rejected.)

We see in others what we struggle to see in ourselves.

The Psychological Mechanism

In psychodynamic theory, projection arises when:

- A thought or feeling is unacceptable to the conscious self
- The psyche externalizes it onto someone else
- This allows the self to maintain coherence — but distorts reality

Over time, projection builds walls, not bridges.

How It Shows Up in Teams

HOW IT SHOWS UP IN TEAMS

Projection	Surface Behavior	Rooted Fear or Pattern
"They don't care about the clients."	Chronic judgment, moral superiority	Fear of one's own burnout or detachment
"They always attack me."	Defensive posture in every conversation	Past wounds of criticism or abandonment
"She's too emotional."	Dismissive behavior	Internalized shame about one's own emotions
"He's so passive-aggressive."	Retaliation or gossip	Repressed anger and lack of boundary skills

The Healing Begins with a Mirror

Healing Circles work because they hold a nonjudgmental mirror up to the group.

Participants are guided gently to:

- Reflect on what triggers them
- Explore what that trigger represents

- Separate the other person's behavior from their own reaction to it
- Reclaim power through insight and choice

"When I stopped making Rafi the villain, I saw how much I've been avoiding conflict. That's mine to face." — Tasha, post-Circle

The Four Layers of Projection

1. Conscious Layer

- Recognition of irritation or tension
- Initial awareness of discomfort
- First impulse: "They're the problem"

2. Pre-Conscious Layer

- Activation of a schema or belief:
  - "I'm never respected"
  - "No one values my voice"
- Pattern of seeing this across multiple relationships

3. Unconscious Layer

- Hidden wounds (e.g., childhood invalidation, betrayal, humiliation)
- Defense mechanisms to avoid re-experiencing emotional pain
- Projection becomes survival — not sabotage

4. Existential Layer

- The invitation: "Now that I know this, who do I choose to be?"
- Reclaiming authorship of internal experience
- Choosing to show up with integrity, curiosity, and humility

Circle Dialogue Practice: Naming the Mirror

In the Circle, we use a practice called "Naming the Mirror."

Participants reflect on:

- A recent workplace irritation
- The feeling it provoked
- A personal experience that mirrors the trigger
- A self-aspect that might be involved

"When I judged her as bossy, what I really couldn't face was how much I silence myself."

This allows conflict to transform from confrontation into compassionate discovery.

Reflection Prompts

- Who at work triggers you the most?
- What feeling do they evoke in you?
- Where else in your life have you felt that way?
- What might this person be reflecting back to you?
- What are you being called to heal within?

FROM PROJECTION TO RESPONSIBILITY

Step	Old Reaction	New Practice
Triggered by someone	React with blame or withdrawal	Pause and notice the emotional charge
Make assumptions	"They're wrong, I'm right"	Ask: What might I be seeing in them that's mine?
Act out or avoid	Gossip, tension, resignation	Engage with curiosity and accountability
Repeat the pattern	Same conflict, different person	Commit to new response with awareness

Tool: The Projection Reversal Worksheet

1. Identify the behavior that triggered you.

2. Name the feeling you had in response.

3. Ask: When else in my life have I felt this way?

4. Reflect: Is there any part of me that shows up this way?

5. Choose: How can I respond with self-responsibility?

This worksheet is used during Circle reflection and in supervision follow-up.

Commitment Practice

Choose one person you've been in conflict with — or emotionally avoiding.

Complete the Projection Reversal Worksheet.

Then choose one compassionate act toward that person this week:

- A kind word
- A check-in
- A moment of pause before judgment
- A shared coffee or moment of listening

Let yourself see them not as a threat — but as a mirror.

Scientific References

- Freud, A. (1936). The Ego and the Mechanisms of Defence. International Universities Press.
- Jung, C. G. (1959). The Archetypes and the Collective Unconscious. Princeton University Press.
- Kernberg, O. F. (1975). Borderline Conditions and Pathological Narcissism.
- Siegel, D. J. (2010). Mindsight: The New Science of Personal Transformation.
- Yalom, I. D. (1995). The Theory and Practice of Group Psychotherapy.
- Holmes, J. (2010). Exploring Insecurity: Towards an Attachment-Informed Psychoanalytic Psychotherapy.

Chapter 6 — From Reaction to Responsibility

The power of the pause — and how accountability begins within

"Between stimulus and response, there is a space. In that space is our power to choose our response. In our response lies our growth and our freedom." — Viktor Frankl

Scene: Thursday, Staff Meeting Debrief, 11:06 a.m.

Luis, a housing case manager, clenched his jaw during the meeting. The new policy changes had just been announced.

Luis: "No one asked for our input. Again. What's the point of pretending this is collaborative?"

Sandra, a newly promoted supervisor, started to respond — defensively. But then she stopped. Took a breath. And said:

Sandra: "I hear you. And I can see this feels like a repeat of something. Would you be willing to unpack this together later today?"

Luis nodded.

That moment — the pause, the breath, the choice — shifted the entire room.

What Is Responsibility, Really?

Responsibility is not blame. It is not compliance. It is not passivity in the face of hierarchy. Responsibility is the capacity to respond — rather than react. It is grounded in awareness, agency, and alignment with one's values.

In organizational psychology, response flexibility is one of the key predictors of adaptive functioning, resilience, and long-term collaboration (Siegel, 2007; Gross, 2014).

The Neuroscience of Reaction

When confronted with threat (real or perceived), the brain rapidly activates:

- The amygdala (emotional alarm system)
- Suppresses prefrontal cortex (executive functioning, rational thought)
- Triggers fight, flight, freeze, or fawn behaviors

In these moments, we regress to survival strategies — not because we are weak, but because we are wired for protection.

However, with awareness and practice, we can interrupt this automaticity.

Circle-Based Practice: The Power of the Pause

One of the most transformative moments in the SWEET Healing Circle is the collective pause — when staff are asked to breathe, notice, and choose before speaking. This moment interrupts the reaction chain. It creates space. And in that space, transformation becomes possible.

"If I had spoken immediately, I would've blamed. But because I waited, I saw myself." — Healing Circle participant

The Four Layers of Reaction

1. Conscious Layer

- Observable behaviors: eye rolls, raised voice, sarcasm
- Practices: Breathwork, somatic grounding, nonverbal awareness

2. Pre-Conscious Layer

- Activated schemas: "I'm being dismissed," "I'm invisible," "I'm being controlled"
- Practices: Thought labeling, pattern interruption, schema inquiry

3. Unconscious Layer

- Reenactments of old wounds: parental invalidation, peer exclusion, unresolved shame
- Practices: Free association, symbolic exploration, facilitated dialogue

4. Existential Layer

- The fundamental choice: Who am I becoming in this moment?
- Practices: Value-based action, conscious ownership, moral reorientation

FROM REACTION TO RESPONSIBILITY

Stage	Default Reaction	Responsible Action
Trigger	Emotional Flooding	Pause and Breathe
Narrative Activation	"They're attacking me"	"What belief is being activated?"
Behavioral Response	Withdrawal or escalation	Thoughtful engagement or redirection
Meaning Attribution	"They don't care about me"	"What story am I telling myself right now?"
Existential Choice	Resignation or revenge	"What do I choose to embody?"

Tool: The STOP Technique for Staff Dynamics

S – Stop and take one conscious breath

T – Take notice of your thoughts, feelings, body state

O – Observe the story you are constructing

P – Proceed with intention, not reaction

Used in the Circle, this tool becomes a behavioral anchor for staff under stress.

Responsibility as a Cultural Lever

When responsibility becomes a shared practice, the organizational culture begins to shift:

- Blame decreases
- Curiosity increases
- Defensive energy dissolves
- Teams operate from shared mission, not shared wounds

This shift cannot be forced. It is to be modeled, practiced, and reinforced through collective reflection.

Reflection Prompts

- What was your last reactive moment at work?
- What was your body doing? Your thoughts?
- What schema or belief might have been triggered?
- What could you have chosen instead?
- What would it mean for you to respond — and not react — as a daily practice?

Commitment Practice

This week, identify one high-trigger relationship or situation at work.

Use the **STOP** Technique the next time you feel emotionally activated.

Then Journal:

- What happened?
- What did I notice?
- What did I choose?
- How do I feel about the outcome?

Repeat daily for seven days. Watch what shifts.

Scientific References

- Frankl, V. E. (1946). Man's Search for Meaning. Beacon Press.
- Siegel, D. J. (2007). The Mindful Brain. Norton & Company.
- Gross, J. J. (2014). Emotion Regulation: Conceptual Foundations. Handbook of Emotion Regulation.
- Baumeister, R. F., & Heatherton, T. F. (1996). Self-regulation failure: An overview. Psychological Inquiry, 7(1), 1–15.
- Schwartz, R. (2021). No Bad Parts: Healing Trauma and Restoring Wholeness with the Internal Family Systems Model. Sounds True.

Chapter 7 — The Inside-Out Leader

How self-aware leaders shift entire cultures without force

"The leader is not the loudest voice in the room. The leader is the clearest mirror."— *SWEET Institute*

Scene: Leadership Circle, Friday 4:22 p.m.

Malika, the agency director from Chapter 3, sat in her office after attending her first Healing Circle.

She wasn't taking notes. She was staring at her reflection in the darkened window.

"I've been asking my team to show up differently," she whispered.

"But I haven't been asking that of myself."

The Circle hadn't just shown her her staff.

It had shown her herself.

What Is Inside-Out Leadership?

Inside-Out Leadership is the SWEET model of leading by:

1. Self-awareness
2. Self-regulation
3. Integrity of word and behavior
4. Relationship to meaning and mission

This is not performative. It is not perfectionistic.

It is transformational leadership rooted in psychological integration.

"You can't take people where you haven't gone." — *Adapted from John Maxwell*

The Layers of Leadership

Just as individuals change through the four layers (conscious, pre-conscious, unconscious, existential), so do leaders.

1. Conscious Layer

– Visible Behavior

- Modeling punctuality, consistency, and professionalism
- Practicing stress regulation, presence, and feedback
- Prioritizing breath, body, and boundaries

2. Pre-Conscious Layer

– Internal Patterns

- Exploring inherited beliefs:
  - "Leadership means being strong."
  - "If I don't control everything, it'll fall apart."
  - "I must be liked to be respected."
- Unlearning distorted leadership identities

3. Unconscious Layer

– Repressed Stories

- Transference from staff to leader and vice versa
- Unresolved fears of failure, humiliation, inadequacy
- Projection of parental dynamics onto supervisees

4. Existential Layer

– Identity, Meaning, and Freedom

- Reclaiming leadership as a choice
- Clarifying your leadership philosophy
- Aligning behavior with values, not reactions
- Asking: "What kind of leader do I want to become?"

INSIDE-OUT VS OUTSIDE-IN LEADERSHIP

Outside-In Leadership	Inside-Out Leadership
Reactive and positional	Responsive and relational
Driven by fear, optics, pressure	Guided by values, vision, purpose
Controls with rules	Leads through trust and example
Uses authority	Uses awareness
Avoids conflict	Engages with presence and clarity

Why It Matters in Healing Circles

Healing Circles work best when leadership participates as equals, not overseers.

When staff see a leader:

- Owning their own patterns
- Taking a breath instead of reacting
- Naming a fear or blind spot
- Offering a genuine apology
- Listening without defense

…trust is built faster than any memo ever written.

Leadership becomes a lived model of healing.

The Role of Emotional Regulation

The most critical leadership skill in high-stress environments is nervous system regulation.

When a leader walks into the room, the room either constricts or relaxes. The team either flinches or exhales.

Why? Because humans are wired for co-regulation. A regulated leader leads a regulated system. A dysregulated leader leads a fearful system. This isn't personal. It's biological.

Reflection Prompts

- How do you enter the room as a leader?
- What emotional residue do you leave behind when you exit?
- When have you reacted instead of responded?
- What would it look like to lead with curiosity, not control?

Tool: The Leadership Mirror Inventory

A weekly check-in tool for Inside-Out Leaders:

THE LEADERSHIP MIRROR INVENTORY

Domain	Check-in	Scale (1-10)	Reflection Question
Presence	Was I mentally and emotionally present this week?		
Pattern Awareness	Did I lead from past fear or present clarity?		
Regulation	How well did I manage emotional triggers?		
Repair	Did I apologize or reconnect when needed?		
Purpose	Did I align decisions with our mission?		

Case Study: Jacob Becomes a Mirror

Jacob, the skeptical housing coordinator from Chapter 3, later became a team lead. He resisted joining the Healing Circle. But once in it, he broke open. "I realized I'd become what I resented — an authority who didn't listen."

Six months later, his team had the lowest turnover and highest engagement scores in the agency.

Not because he changed them. Because he changed himself.

Commitment Practice

This week, practice one Inside-Out Leadership behavior:

- Admit a mistake
- Ask a staff member how they're really doing
- Regulate before responding
- Share your learning process openly
- Show vulnerability without self-pity

Then reflect:

What shifted in the room because I showed up differently?

Scientific References

- Goleman, D. (1995). Emotional Intelligence. Bantam Books.
- Siegel, D. J. (2010). Mindsight: The New Science of Personal Transformation.
- Bass, B. M., & Riggio, R. E. (2006). Transformational Leadership.
- Porges, S. W. (2011). The Polyvagal Theory.
- Schein, E. H. (2010). Organizational Culture and Leadership.
- Greenleaf, R. K. (1977). Servant Leadership. Paulist Press.

Chapter 8 — A Circle Culture

What happens when reflection becomes part of the system

"Culture is not created by mission statements. Culture is created by what people do when stress is high and nobody's watching." — *SWEET Institute*

Scene: Monday Morning, 10:03 a.m.

It was the third Monday of the month at Unity, a mid-sized human services agency. At 10 a.m. sharp, the agency's community room filled with a mix of case managers, peer specialists, administrative staff, nurses, and program directors.

There were no PowerPoints. No announcements. No "agenda."

Just chairs, in a circle.

And a shared understanding:

- This is where we remember who we are.

What Is a Circle Culture?

A Circle Culture is what happens when an organization makes Healing Circles:

- Regular (quarterly, monthly, or even weekly)
- Accessible (open to all levels of staff)
- Supported (by leadership and structure)
- Modeled (by those in positions of influence)

It's a culture where people know:

- There will be a space to speak without fear
- Reflection is not a luxury — it's a necessity
- Relationships matter as much as results
- Healing is everyone's responsibility

Why It Works

When Circles become a rhythmic part of organizational life, several things begin to shift:

1. Psychological safety increases (Edmondson, 1999)
2. Silos begin to dissolve
3. Accountability becomes relational, not punitive
4. Staff retention improves (because connection improves)
5. The mission becomes embodied — not just recited

*"It's no longer just the work I do. It's the people I do it with." —
Healing Circle participant*

The Four Layers of Circle Culture

Just like individuals and leaders, organizations transform through the four layers:

1. Conscious Layer

– Systems and Structure

- Scheduling regular Circles
- Training facilitators internally
- Tracking participation and engagement
- Creating opt-in reflection spaces post-crisis

2. Pre-Conscious Layer

– Unspoken Norms

- Challenging the culture of busyness and avoidance
- Dismantling fear-based communication norms
- Bringing light to patterns of silence, blame, or disengagement

3. *Unconscious Layer*

– Organizational Trauma

- Acknowledging past leadership wounds
- Repairing historical injustices or favoritism
- Honoring grief, burnout, or collective ruptures

4. *Existential Layer*

– Organizational Identity

- Revisiting the why as a team
- Inviting every staff member to own the mission
- Asking: "What kind of organization do we want to become together?"

FROM EVENT TO ECOSYSTEM

One-Time Event	Circle Culture
"Nice experience"	Ongoing self-reflection and accountability
Led only by external staff	Internal facilitators across departments
Seen as a luxury	Seen as essential to performance and wellness
Optional and isolated	Integrated into onboarding, supervision, team meetings

Case Study: Open House Turns the Curve

At Open House, Healing Circles began as an experimental staff intervention. Within a year:

- Turnover decreased by 37%
- Internal promotion increased by 24%
- Conflicts were more often resolved informally
- Staff reported increased meaning and belonging

- Supervisors reported fewer escalations and greater cohesion

"Before the Circle, we were always firefighting. After the Circle, we started fireproofing." — *Program Director, Open House*

Reflection Prompts

- Is there currently space for your team to reflect together — safely, regularly, and deeply?

- What conversations are your staff longing to have, but afraid to initiate?

- What's keeping your agency from being more human, more united, more mission-driven?

THE CIRCLE CULTURE READINESS CHECKLIST

Element	In Place?	Next Steps
Regular Circle schedule		
Trained facilitators		
Support from leadership		
Integration with staff development		
Follow-up reflection and support practices		

Organizations can use this as a launchpad for culture strategy.

Commitment Practice

If you're in a position to influence culture:

1. Schedule one Healing Circle in the next 30 days
2. Invite people across levels — not just leaders
3. Debrief with a "One Thing" — one insight or action each person is taking
4. Reflect on what shifts — in tone, energy, alignment

Culture doesn't change through policy.

It changes through presence.

Scientific References

- Edmondson, A. C. (1999). Psychological Safety and Learning Behavior in Work Teams. Administrative Science Quarterly, 44(2), 350–383.
- Schein, E. H. (2010). Organizational Culture and Leadership. Jossey-Bass.
- Brown, B. (2012). Daring Greatly. Penguin Random House.
- West, M. A., & Dawson, J. F. (2012). Employee Engagement and NHS Performance. The King's Fund.
- Wenger, E. (1998). Communities of Practice: Learning, Meaning, and Identity. Cambridge University Press.

Part III

From Insight to Integration

Chapter 9 — From Information to Integration

Why most trainings fail — and how Circles bridge the knowing-doing gap

"Information is not transformation. Insight is not implementation. Knowing is not doing."

— SWEET Institute

Scene: Leadership Roundtable, Tuesday 3:30 p.m.

Nathan, the executive director of an award-winning non-profit, leaned back in his chair.

Nathan: "We've sent staff to trauma-informed training, racial equity seminars, even resilience workshops. But two months later, we're back to the same patterns."

The room was quiet.

Then Alison, the clinical lead, replied: "That's because we're teaching from the outside in. And what people need is the inside out."

Why Training Doesn't Equal Change

Most trainings:

- Emphasize information transfer
- Prioritize intellectual understanding
- Treat behavior as outcomes, not symptoms
- Ignore the psychological architecture behind resistance, fatigue, and relapse

Result?

Short-term inspiration. Long-term inertia.

What Integration Requires

Real change requires more than insight.

It requires an experience that touches all four layers:

Layer	Training Outcome	Healing Circle Outcome
Conscious	Conceptual awareness	Behavioral awareness + anchored practices
Pre-Conscious	"That's interesting…"	"That's my story — and I'm ready to change it."
Unconscious	Ignored or bypassed	Gently surfaced and explored through symbol + emotion
Existential	Not addressed	Meaning reconnected, ownership reclaimed

The Science of Implementation Failure

Research from implementation science (Fixsen et al., 2005) shows that:

- Training alone yields only 10–20% of behavior change
- Without ongoing coaching and reflection, that number drops further
- Change only sustains when people are emotionally engaged and held accountable by community

This is exactly what the Healing Circle does.

It is not a one-way delivery. It is a whole-person invitation.

The Healing Circle Implementation Framework

The SWEET Healing Circle follows a four-stage integration arc:

1. Disruption

The Circle introduces a new experience of self and others — one that interrupts business as usual.

"I saw a pattern I never noticed before. It was hard — but freeing."

2. Reflection

Participants are guided to inquire deeply:

- "What do I feel?"
- "What is this really about?"
- "What belief is this activating?"

This moves learning from the head to the heart.

3. Commitment

Each Circle ends with a clear, self-chosen commitment — not to the facilitator, but to one's own growth.

4. Integration

Follow-up tools, team check-ins, and supervisor conversations help embed the change over time.

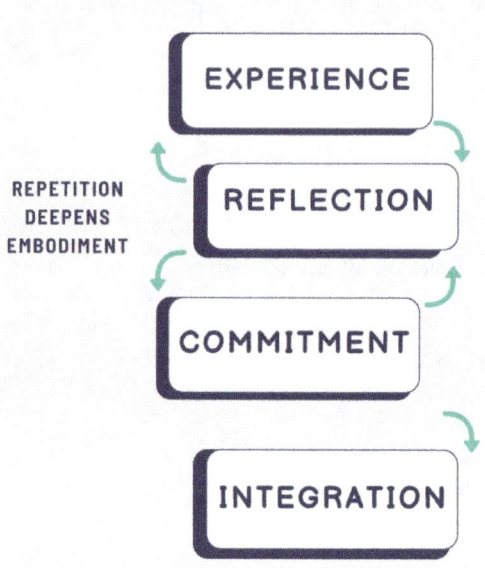

The Integration Spiral

Why Insight Isn't Enough

You can know that you tend to withdraw during conflict…

…and still do it.

You can understand trauma…

…and still retraumatize others with your tone.

You can teach accountability…

…and still lead from fear and control.

What we know doesn't change us.

What we practice — and repeat — does.

FROM INSIGHT TO ACTION PLANNER

Insight	Trigger Moment	New Response I Am Committing To
"I get defensive when challenged"	Supervision feedback session	Pause, breathe, respond with curiosity
"I don't speak up in meetings"	Monday morning huddles	Write one thing down and share it aloud
"I avoid team conflict"	After incident debriefs	Name the tension and invite conversation

Use this tool weekly to bridge the gap between awareness and embodiment.

Reflection Prompts

- What is one thing you know... but haven't yet embodied?
- What gets in the way of your integration — fear? fatigue? habit?
- What structure of support could help you close the gap between knowing and doing?

Commitment Practice

This week, take one insight from your Healing Circle — or your life — and:

1. Identify the behavior or habit it relates to
2. Write down a new response or practice
3. Tell one person who can hold you gently accountable
4. Practice it at least once — and reflect on the result

Transformation happens one response at a time.

Scientific References

- Fixsen, D. L., et al. (2005). Implementation Research: A Synthesis of the Literature. University of South Florida.
- Kolb, D. A. (1984). Experiential Learning. Prentice-Hall.
- Prochaska, J. O., & DiClemente, C. C. (1983). Stages of Change Model.
- Mezirow, J. (1991). Transformative Dimensions of Adult Learning.
- Kegan, R., & Lahey, L. L. (2009). Immunity to Change.
- Bandura, A. (1977). Social Learning Theory. Prentice-Hall.

Chapter 10 — The Agency as a Healing System

What it means to build an organization that heals from the inside out

"An agency is not just a collection of staff. It is a system of relationships. And systems can either wound — or heal." — *SWEET Institute*

Scene: The Exit Interview, 4:40 p.m.

Rafi, the care coordinator from earlier chapters, sat across from Malika, the agency director.

Malika: "Rafi, before you go, can I ask—what made you stay this long?"

Rafi: "Honestly? I almost left a dozen times. But the Circle… changed me. It changed how I see people. How I see myself."

He paused.

"I realized I wasn't just doing a job. I was part of a place where healing actually happened — not just for the residents, but for us."

From Program to Pathway

Most agencies are trained to think in terms of:

- Programs
- Outcomes
- Services
- Deliverables

But beneath it all lies a more radical truth:

Every agency is a healing system — or a system that perpetuates harm.

- Through its relationships
- Through its norms
- Through how it treats the staff who do the work
- Through how it responds to pain — not just in clients, but in itself

What Is a Healing System?

A healing system is not perfect.

It is not free of conflict.

It is not always calm.

But it is:

- Reflective
- Accountable
- Human
- Alive

A healing system is one that recognizes that everyone is a client of the mission — including the staff.

It understands that:

- Trauma is reenacted when power is misused
- Burnout is not a failure of resilience, but of support
- Staff disconnection is not laziness — it's loss of meaning
- Reconnection is to be modeled, not mandated

The Four Layers of Healing Systems

1. Conscious Layer

– Policies and Practices

- Wellness check-ins
- Circle scheduling
- Debriefs and peer support
- Supervision that includes reflection

2. Pre-Conscious Layer

– Culture and Conditioning

- What is celebrated?
- What is silenced?
- What behaviors are reinforced (even unintentionally)?
- What norms are unspoken, but real?

3. Unconscious Layer

– Institutional Memory

- Historical traumas: layoffs, racism, leadership harm
- Intergenerational wounds in agency culture
- The residue of what was never acknowledged

"This isn't the first time we've felt ignored. It's a pattern." — *Staff member, post-Circle*

4. Existential Layer

– Organizational Soul

- Why do we exist?
- Who are we becoming?
- What legacy are we leaving?
- How do we define success — not just in numbers, but in lives?

THE AGENCY AS A HEALING SYSTEM

Layer	Agency Expression
Conscious	Structure, strategy, HR, policy
Pre-Conscious	Culture, tone, norms, staff behavior
Unconscious	Historical wounds, unspoken fears
Existential	Mission, meaning, moral leadership

Healing systems attend to all four.

How the Healing Circle Supports Systems Change

- Surfaces suppressed dynamics
- Humanizes leadership
- Makes space for grief, not just performance
- Bridges departments and silos
- Reconnects people to purpose
- Reinforces "we" over "us vs. them"

"We stopped being just programs. We became people again." — Supervisor, Circle participant

Reflection Prompts

- Where in your agency do people feel emotionally safe? Where do they flinch?
- What legacy of unacknowledged pain might be living in the walls?

- What new norm would you want to initiate — even if quietly — starting this week?
- What would it mean for your agency to be a place of healing, not just services?

Tool: The Healing System Audit

Invite leadership teams to assess each layer:

THE HEALING SYSTEM AUDIT

Layer	Healing Practices in Place	What Needs Strengthening?
Conscious	Yes/No	E.g., reflective supervision
Pre-Conscious	Yes/No	E.g., addressing silence or fear norms
Unconscious	Yes/No	E.g., reckoning with leadership turnover
Existential	Yes/No	E.g., re-rooting in the original mission

This tool is best used in leadership retreats or Circle-inspired strategy sessions.

Commitment Practice

As an agency leader, team member, or change agent:

1. Identify one layer you can influence (conscious, pre-conscious, unconscious, or existential)
2. Choose one action you'll take this month to strengthen that layer
3. Tell one person who can support and witness your commitment
4. Schedule a time to reflect on the impact

Healing happens systemically — when one part heals, the whole shifts.

Scientific References

- Schein, E. H. (2010). Organizational Culture and Leadership. Jossey-Bass.
- Kegan, R., & Lahey, L. L. (2009). Immunity to Change. Harvard Business Press.
- Edmondson, A. (2019). The Fearless Organization. Wiley.
- Brown, B. (2021). Atlas of the Heart. Random House.
- Porges, S. W. (2011). The Polyvagal Theory. Norton.
- Gopnik, A. (2020). The Gardener and the Carpenter. Farrar, Straus and Giroux.

Closing Words

You don't need to fix your agency. You don't need to perfect your team. You don't need to heal everyone's wounds. You just need to start — with one Circle, One pattern, One conversation, One choice to be present.

Because healing isn't abstract. It begins here. In this room. In this body. In this system.

With you.

Epilogue: You Were Always the Circle

You have read the stories. You've seen the patterns. You've traveled through the four layers — of behavior, belief, memory, and meaning. You've sat in the Circle, even if only in your mind. And now, here you are. At the threshold.

The work doesn't end here. It begins where you are — in the next conversation, in the next moment you choose not to react. In the breath you take instead of raising your voice. In the compassion you offer to someone who you think may not "deserve" it. In the pause between your knowing and your doing.

This is the real Circle. Not the one on the calendar. The one in your consciousness. Because you are the culture. You are the nervous system of your organization. You are the breath, the break in the cycle, the one who remembers. You were always the Circle.

And now, may you carry it forward—with your staff, your leaders, your clients, your family, your mission.

This is not the end. This is the integration. This is the beginning.

Conclusion: The Circle Is the Shift

Every agency wants the same thing.

1. Less turnover.
2. More accountability.
3. Real collaboration.
4. A culture that supports its mission instead of draining it.
5. A team that doesn't just work—but works together.

And yet, most systems focus only on what's visible: outcomes, data, behavior. They miss the invisible: belief, emotion, perception, memory, purpose. That's where the real work lives. That's where the Circle begins.

The SWEET Healing Circle is not a technique. It's not a curriculum. It's not a one-time intervention. It's a return—to the wisdom that lives inside each person. It's a mirror, gently revealing what's been hidden but ready to be seen. It's a breath—a sacred space where blame dissolves and responsibility rises. It's a culture-shaping ritual that says: We care not only about what you do. We care about how you're doing.

This book was not written to be admired. It was written to be used. Start with one Circle. Start with one pause. Start with one relationship you're willing to approach differently.

Because when you shift a relationship, you shift a system. And when you heal a system, you change the world.

Invitation to the Reader

You've taken this journey with us — through stories, science, reflection, and soul. Now we invite you to take it further. Don't leave this book on the shelf. Bring it to your team. Bring it into supervision. Bring it to your next Circle. Bring it into the way you lead, the way you listen, the way you respond. You are no longer waiting for someone else to shift the culture. You are the culture.

Reflection + Call to Action

We invite you to pause and reflect on these three questions:

1. What is one relationship I want to transform?
2. What is one pattern I am ready to release?
3. What is one action I will take this week to lead from the inside out?

Write them down. Share them with a colleague. Post them on your wall. Make them real.

Then, schedule a Circle. Start a conversation. Use the tools. Lead with your breath. You don't need to be perfect. You just need to be present.

Help Us Spread the Healing

If this book moved you, helped you, challenged you, or offered clarity, we'd be honored if you left a review. Your words help others find this work. Your feedback helps leaders say yes. Your voice helps Healing Circles reach more teams, more systems, more lives.

Please take two minutes to leave a review on Amazon, Goodreads, or wherever you purchased the book. Because the more voices rise, the more the Circle expands.

With gratitude and shared purpose,

The SWEET Institute
Transforming the system, one relationship at a time.

Final Acknowledgments

This book was born not in solitude, but in community. It was built in conversation, in reflection, in shared tears and break-throughs, in sacred silence and bold truth-telling — in Circles that became sanctuaries.

To the people who sit in rooms of tension and still choose kindness — thank you.

To the leaders who pause before reacting and choose presence over power — thank you.

To the teams who have dared to speak, to listen, to forgive, and to begin again — thank you.

You have shown us what healing looks like when it's no longer an idea, but a way of being.

To the advisors and stewards of the SWEET Institute, your unwavering belief in inside-out transformation has changed thousands of lives. Thank you for choosing this path.

To every reader holding this book, whether you're leading a system or just trying to hold yourself together at work:

You are not alone. You are the system. You are the beginning of the shift. This book is our offering. You — and the people you serve — are our why.

With gratitude and deep respect,

Mardoche Sidor, MD
Alison Dockery, PhD
Karen Dubin, PhD, LCSW
SWEET Institute

Reader Integration Toolkit

A Practical Guide to Applying the SWEET Healing Circle in Your Life, Work, and Leadership

How to Use This Toolkit

This Toolkit is designed to help you:

- Move from insight to implementation
- Apply the SWEET Healing Circle principles in every-day work life
- Transform relationships, team culture, and your leadership from the inside out
- Sustain the change over time — with structure, clarity, and compassion

You can use this Toolkit individually, with your team, in supervision, or to prepare your agency for Circles.

SECTION 1: The Four-Layer Reflection Map

Use this tool to reflect on a challenge, relationship, or recurring workplace pattern:

THE FOUR-LAYER REFLECTION MAP

Layer	Reflection Questions
Conscious	What am I doing or not doing in this situation? What habits are involved?
Pre-Conscious	What patterns, beliefs, or stories are influencing my behavior?
Unconscious	What past experiences might be shaping my reaction here?
Existential	Who do I want to become in this relationship? What meaning do I choose?

SECTION 2: Projection Reversal Worksheet

When triggered by someone at work:

1. What did they do or say that bothered me?
2. What emotion did that bring up in me?
3. When else in my life have I felt that way?
4. What might this person be reflecting back to me about myself?
5. What am I willing to own, heal, or change?

SECTION 3: The STOP Technique for Response over Reaction

Use this tool in real-time moments of stress or conflict:

S – Stop

T – Take a breath

O – Observe your thoughts, body, and impulse

P – Proceed from awareness, not habit

Practice this daily — especially in leadership moments.

SECTION 4: Insight to Action Planner

For every major insight you gain, ask:

INSIGHT TO ACTION PLANNER

Insight	Behavior Change	When Will I Practice It?
Example: "I avoid feedback conversations"	"Schedule one honest 1:1 per week"	Mondays at 10 a.m.

Use this planner weekly. Transformation happens in rhythm.

SECTION 5: One Commitment Card (For You or Your Team)

Fill in and keep visible. Share it with a colleague or your team.

One pattern I'm releasing:

One behavior I'm choosing:

One person I'm repairing with:

One value I will lead with:

One reason I still choose this work:

SECTION 6: Circle Culture Readiness Checklist (Leadership Tool)

CIRCLE CULTURE READINESS CHECKLIST

Element	In Place?	Next Step
Regular Circle schedule	Yes/No	
Internal facilitators or external support	Yes/No	
Debriefs and supervision integration	Yes/No	
Leadership modeling of reflection	Yes/No	

Use this as part of annual planning or cultural transformation strategy.

SECTION 7: 21-Day Circle Integration Challenge

For 21 days, commit to:

- Practicing one SWEET principle daily (see prompts below)
- Noticing your default patterns — without judgment
- Choosing one new response — each day

Daily Practice Prompts:

- Today, I will respond instead of react by…
- Today, I will reflect instead of blame by…
- Today, I will reconnect to the mission by…
- Today, I will breathe before speaking when…
- Today, I will see the person behind the behavior in…

SECTION 8: Healing System Audit (For Executive and Leadership Teams)

Assess your agency using the Four Layers of Systems:

HEALING SYSTEM AUDIT

Layer	Do We Address This?	Examples / Notes
Conscious	Yes/No	Policies, practices, trainings
Pre-Conscious	Yes/No	Unspoken norms, communication habits
Unconscious	Yes/No	Historic wounds, turnover trauma
Existential	Yes/No	Meaning, shared values, moral alignment

Final Note:

Use this Toolkit slowly. Repeatedly. Reflectively.

Healing is not a sprint. It is a sacred pattern — of remembering, re-choosing, re-aligning.

You don't need to do it all at once. You just need to begin.

Appendix

Appendix A: The Four-Layer Reflection Map

Use this to explore any challenge, conflict, or stuck relationship.

THE FOUR-LAYER REFLECTION MAP

Layer	Questions to Reflect On
Conscious	What am I doing or not doing in this situation? What habits are involved?
Pre-Conscious	What belief or emotional pattern might be driving my behavior here?
Unconscious	What early experiences might be getting reactivated right now?
Existential	What kind of person or leader do I want to become in this moment?

Appendix B: Projection Reversal Worksheet

Use this tool when you feel triggered by someone:

1. What did they do that activated me?
2. What emotion did I feel?
3. Where else in my life have I felt that way?
4. What might this person be reflecting about myself?
5. What do I choose to own, shift, or let go of?

Appendix C: The STOP Technique

To regulate yourself in moments of stress:

S – Stop

T – Take a breath

O – Observe your inner and outer experience

P – Proceed with intention

This tool is simple, powerful, and highly effective in de-escalating staff tension.

Appendix D: Insight to Action Planner

Track your transformation by turning insight into practice:

INSIGHT TO ACTION PLANNER

Insight Gained	Behavior Change	When Will I Apply This?
E.g., "I avoid feedback"	"Schedule 1 honest conversation weekly"	"Tuesdays at 10 a.m."

Appendix E: One Commitment Card

Use this post-Circle or during staff check-ins:

- One pattern I am releasing:
- One behavior I am practicing:
- One person I am reconnecting with:
- One value I will embody:
- One reason I still choose this work:

Appendix F: Circle Culture Readiness Checklist

Assess your agency's readiness to integrate Healing Circles systemically:

CIRCLE CULTURE READINESS CHECKLIST

Component	In Place?	Next Step/Notes
Regular Circle schedule	Yes/No	
Internal or external Circle facilitators	Yes/No	
Circle follow-ups or reflection practices	Yes/No	
Leadership participation and modeling	Yes/No	

Appendix G: 21-Day Integration Challenge

Try this on your own or with your team:

For 21 days, complete one prompt daily:

- Today, I will choose curiosity over control by…
- Today, I will respond instead of react by…
- Today, I will reconnect with my "why" by…
- Today, I will hold space for someone else's growth by…
- Today, I will practice presence when…

Appendix H: Healing System Audit (Leadership Tool)

For use in executive meetings or planning retreats.

HEALING SYSTEM AUDIT

Layer	Do We Address This?	Examples / Opportunities
Conscious	Yes/No	e.g., reflective supervision, team rituals
Pre-Conscious	Yes/No	e.g., feedback culture, staff storytelling
Unconscious	Yes/No	e.g., unhealed staff dynamics, leadership shifts
Existential	Yes/No	e.g., purpose-driven decisions, value alignment

Final Words

Transformation doesn't happen in one Circle. It happens in daily practice. In team habits. In quiet choices.

This Toolkit is your bridge from learning to living. May it support your leadership, your relationships, and your collective mission.

The Circle continues.

Scientific Reference Index

Chapter 1: The Staff Are Not Okay

- Maslach, C., Jackson, S. E., & Leiter, M. P. (2001). Job Burnout. Annual Review of Psychology, 52(1), 397–422.
- American Psychological Association (2022). Workforce Wellbeing Survey.
- Edmondson, A. C. (1999). Psychological Safety and Learning Behavior in Work Teams. Administrative Science Quarterly, 44(2), 350–383.
- Jung, C. G. (1959). The Archetypes and the Collective Unconscious. Princeton University Press.
- Van der Kolk, B. (2014). The Body Keeps the Score. Viking.

Chapter 2: Conflict Is Not the Problem

- Lieberman, M. D., & Eisenberger, N. I. (2007). The Neural Bases of Social Pain: Evidence for Shared Representations with Physical Pain. Nature Reviews Neuroscience, 8(3), 203–212.
- Jung, C. G. (1959). The Archetypes and the Collective Unconscious. Princeton University Press.
- Yalom, I. D. (1995). The Theory and Practice of Group Psychotherapy. Basic Books.
- Siegel, D. J. (2007). The Mindful Brain. W. W. Norton.
- Gross, J. J. (2014). Emotion Regulation: Conceptual Foundations. Handbook of Emotion Regulation.

Chapter 3: The SWEET Healing Circle Model

- Kolb, D. A. (1984). Experiential Learning. Prentice-Hall.
- Doidge, N. (2007). The Brain That Changes Itself. Penguin.
- Porges, S. W. (2011). The Polyvagal Theory. W. W. Norton.

- Yalom, I. D. (1995). The Theory and Practice of Group Psychotherapy. Basic Books.
- Siegel, D. J. (2007). The Mindful Brain. W. W. Norton.
- Schein, E. H. (2010). Organizational Culture and Leadership. Jossey-Bass.

Chapter 4: The Four Layers of Transformation

- Beck, A. T., Freeman, A. (1990). Cognitive Therapy of Personality Disorders. Guilford Press.
- Young, J. E., Klosko, J. S. (2003). Schema Therapy: A Practitioner's Guide. Guilford Press.
- Freud, S. (1915). The Unconscious. Standard Edition, 14: 159–215.
- Frankl, V. E. (1946). Man's Search for Meaning. Beacon Press.
- Yalom, I. D. (1980). Existential Psychotherapy. Basic Books.
- Porges, S. W. (2011). The Polyvagal Theory. W. W. Norton.

Chapter 5: Projection at Work

- Freud, A. (1936). The Ego and the Mechanisms of Defence. International Universities Press.
- Jung, C. G. (1959). The Archetypes and the Collective Unconscious. Princeton University Press.
- Kernberg, O. F. (1975). Borderline Conditions and Pathological Narcissism. Jason Aronson.
- Siegel, D. J. (2010). Mindsight: The New Science of Personal Transformation. Bantam.
- Yalom, I. D. (1995). The Theory and Practice of Group Psychotherapy. Basic Books.
- Holmes, J. (2010). Exploring Insecurity: Towards an Attachment-Informed Psychoanalytic Psychotherapy. Routledge.

Chapter 6: From Reaction to Responsibility

- Frankl, V. E. (1946). Man's Search for Meaning. Beacon Press.
- Siegel, D. J. (2007). The Mindful Brain. W. W. Norton.
- Gross, J. J. (2014). Emotion Regulation: Conceptual Foundations. Handbook of Emotion Regulation.
- Baumeister, R. F., & Heatherton, T. F. (1996). Self-Regulation Failure: An Overview. Psychological Inquiry, 7(1), 1–15.
- Schwartz, R. C. (2021). No Bad Parts. Sounds True.

Chapter 7: The Inside-Out Leader

- Goleman, D. (1995). Emotional Intelligence. Bantam Books.
- Siegel, D. J. (2010). Mindsight: The New Science of Personal Transformation. Bantam.
- Bass, B. M., & Riggio, R. E. (2006). Transformational Leadership. Psychology Press.
- Porges, S. W. (2011). The Polyvagal Theory. W. W. Norton.
- Schein, E. H. (2010). Organizational Culture and Leadership. Jossey-Bass.
- Greenleaf, R. K. (1977). Servant Leadership. Paulist Press.

Chapter 8: A Circle Culture

- Edmondson, A. C. (1999). Psychological Safety and Learning Behavior in Work Teams. Administrative Science Quarterly, 44(2), 350–383.
- Schein, E. H. (2010). Organizational Culture and Leadership. Jossey-Bass.
- Brown, B. (2012). Daring Greatly. Penguin Random House.
- West, M. A., & Dawson, J. F. (2012). Employee Engagement and NHS Performance. The King's Fund.

- Wenger, E. (1998). Communities of Practice: Learning, Meaning, and Identity. Cambridge University Press.

Chapter 9: From Information to Integration

- Fixsen, D. L., et al. (2005). Implementation Research: A Synthesis of the Literature. University of South Florida.
- Kolb, D. A. (1984). Experiential Learning. Prentice-Hall.
- Prochaska, J. O., & DiClemente, C. C. (1983). Stages of Change Model.
- Mezirow, J. (1991). Transformative Dimensions of Adult Learning. Jossey-Bass.
- Kegan, R., & Lahey, L. L. (2009). Immunity to Change. Harvard Business Press.
- Bandura, A. (1977). Social Learning Theory. Prentice-Hall.

Chapter 10: The Agency as a Healing System

- Schein, E. H. (2010). Organizational Culture and Leadership. Jossey-Bass.
- Kegan, R., & Lahey, L. L. (2009). Immunity to Change. Harvard Business Press.
- Edmondson, A. (2019). The Fearless Organization. Wiley.
- Brown, B. (2021). Atlas of the Heart. Random House.
- Porges, S. W. (2011). The Polyvagal Theory. W. W. Norton.
- Gopnik, A. (2020). The Gardener and the Carpenter. Farrar, Straus and Giroux.

Recommended Reading

For Deeper Integration, Leadership, and Transformation

Organizational Culture & Healing Systems

- Schein, Edgar H. (2010). Organizational Culture and Leadership.
- Kegan, Robert & Lahey, Lisa L. (2009). Immunity to Change.
- Edmondson, Amy C. (2019). The Fearless Organization.
- Brown, Brené. (2021). Atlas of the Heart.
- West, Michael A. (2021). Compassionate Leadership: Sustaining Wisdom, Humanity, and Presence in Health and Social Care.

Trauma, Neuroscience & Healing

- Van der Kolk, Bessel. (2014). The Body Keeps the Score.
- Porges, Stephen. (2011). The Polyvagal Theory: Neurophysiological Foundations of Emotions, Attachment, Communication, and Self-Regulation.
- Siegel, Daniel J. (2010). Mindsight: The New Science of Personal Transformation.
- Schwartz, Richard C. (2021). No Bad Parts: Healing Trauma and Restoring Wholeness with the Internal Family Systems Model.

Reflection, Responsibility & Self-Leadership

- Frankl, Viktor E. (1946). Man's Search for Meaning.
- Glouberman, Sheila. (2022). The Pause Principle: Leadership and the Power of Presence.
- Goleman, Daniel. (1995). Emotional Intelligence.
- Tolle, Eckhart. (1999). The Power of Now: A Guide to Spiritual Enlightenment.

- Stone, Douglas; Patton, Bruce; Heen, Sheila. (2010). Difficult Conversations.

Psychology of Patterns, Defense, and Change

- Young, Jeffrey; Klosko, Janet. (2003). Schema Therapy: A Practitioner's Guide.
- Yalom, Irvin D. (1995). The Theory and Practice of Group Psychotherapy.
- Mezirow, Jack. (1991). Transformative Dimensions of Adult Learning.
- Jung, Carl G. (1959). The Archetypes and the Collective Unconscious.

Leadership, Dialogue, and Inner Work in Systems

- Wheatley, Margaret. (2002). Turning to One Another: Simple Conversations to Restore Hope to the Future.
- Greenleaf, Robert. (1977). Servant Leadership: A Journey into the Nature of Legitimate Power and Greatness.
- Palmer, Parker. (2000). Let Your Life Speak: Listening for the Voice of Vocation.
- Block, Peter. (2009). Community: The Structure of Belonging.

More from SWEET Institute Publishing

Transformational Books for a Transformational World

At SWEET Institute Publishing, we believe that healing is not just personal — it is professional, systemic, and spiritual. Our books are written to bridge the gap between knowing and doing, between theory and transformation, between systems and souls.

Whether you're a clinician, a leader, an advocate, or a life-long learner — our titles are here to support your journey.

Available Now:

The Power of Belief

How what we believe shapes our identity, our systems, and the world around us — and how to change it.

Coming Soon:

- ### *Before Anything Else, Validate*

  Why validation is the foundation of healing, collaboration, and change — and how to practice it in every interaction.

- ### *The Courage to Care*

  Stories of healing, hope, and the profound wisdom of social work, told through the voices of 50 clinicians.

- ### *How Life Works*

  A dialogue-based journey through life's patterns, lessons, and meaning — for those ready to live on purpose.

- *Freeing Fear*

  A practical and poetic exploration of how fear controls us — and how to reclaim our freedom across all four layers of the mind.

- *Rewriting the Script: Healing Internalized Oppression*

  A powerful guide to recognizing, rewriting, and healing the stories we were never meant to carry.

- *The Simplicity Principle*

  Why breaking things down is the key to learning, healing, and growing in any domain of life.

- *The Clinician's Mirror*

  How projection, pattern, and presence shape our practice — and how to use every encounter as a path to self-discovery.

- *The Anchor Blueprint*

  A new model of care for high-acuity populations — rooted in dignity, depth, and layered healing systems.

Stay Connected

To receive updates, resources, and upcoming releases:

Visit: www.SWEETInstitutePublishing.com

Subscribe: newsletter.sweetinstitute.com

Follow: @SWEETInstitute on LinkedIn, Instagram, and Facebook

About the Authors

Mardoche Sidor, MD

Dr. Mardoche Sidor is a quadruple board-certified psychiatrist, trained in general psychiatry, child and adolescent psychiatry, forensic psychiatry, and addiction psychiatry. He is also trained in public and community psychiatry and geriatric psychiatry. Formerly an Assistant Clinical Professor of Psychiatry at Columbia University, Dr. Sidor is now affiliated with the Columbia University Center for Psychoanalytic Training and Research. He is the founder of the SWEET Institute and currently serves as Medical Director at Urban Pathways in New York City.

Dr. Sidor has dedicated his life to transforming mental health care by integrating scientific rigor, clinical depth, and spiritual insight. He is a prolific author, national and international speaker, and thought leader in inside-out systems transformation. His work blends psychoanalysis, neuroscience, trauma healing, and applied philosophy to promote sustainable change across individuals, teams, and institutions.

Alison Dockery, PhD

Dr. Alison Dockery is a clinical psychologist, researcher, and educator with a passion for turning systems of survival into systems of healing. With deep expertise in adult development, organizational dynamics, and psychological integration, she has supported teams and leaders across the nonprofit, healthcare, and educational sectors to become more reflective, accountable, and purpose-aligned.

Dr. Dockery is known for her grounded, human-centered approach to complexity. Her work integrates schema theory, systems thinking, and trauma-responsive leadership to help individuals and institutions move beyond performative reform and into true transformation.

Karen Dubin, PhD, LCSW

Dr. Karen Dubin is a licensed clinical social worker, therapist, educator, and senior faculty member at the SWEET Institute. With over two decades of experience in direct practice, clinical supervision, and systems change, she brings both relational depth and practical clarity to the work of healing.

Karen is a writer, speaker, and Circle facilitator who leads from a place of fierce compassion. Her teachings center around narrative integration, projection, and the clinician's inner life — always with an eye toward justice, dignity, and whole-person care.

SWEET Institute

SWEET Institute (Supporting Wellbeing, Empowerment, Education, and Training) is a global education and transformation platform for clinicians, educators, and organizational leaders. Through live courses, Healing Circles, publishing, and systems consultation, SWEET empowers individuals and institutions to move from information to integration, from burnout to meaning, and from fear to freedom.

Learn more at www.SWEETInstitute.com.